for Women

Mary Barrett

**Dedicated to my sister Geraldine Casbon,
who in spite of living with kidney failure
has inspired all who know her with
her ability to praise God at all times.**

First published 2003
Copyright © 2003
Reprinted 2003, 2007, 2009 and 2010

All rights reserved. No part of this publication
may be reproduced in any form without prior
permission from the publisher.

British Library Cataloguing in Publication Data.
A catalogue record for this book is available
from the British Library.

ISBN 1-903921-05-8

Published by
Autumn House
Grantham, Lincs.
Printed in Thailand.

INTRODUCTION

'Be joyful always; pray continually; give thanks in all circumstances,
for this is God's will for you in Christ Jesus.'
1 Thessalonians 5:16-18.

'Rejoice in the Lord always. I will say it again: Rejoice!'
Philippians 4:4

The Bible tells us to rejoice always. But that is not an easy thing to do.
Very often when we praise God, we end up saying the same
thing over and over again.
This little book is designed to help you praise God in different
ways, by using a scripture verse as a springboard for a
praise thought to God.
Use one each day and see your appreciation for God grow as you
praise him for the many marvellous aspects of his character.

Happy praising!

All texts are taken from the
New International Version unless indicated.
CIV = Children's International Version
GNB = Good News Bible
KJV = King James Version
MGE = The Message
NLT = New Living Translation

Psalm 23:2

'He makes me lie down in green pastures,
he leads me beside quiet waters,
he restores my soul.'

Praise God
*for the times in your life
when he tenderly takes you by the hand
and leads you to a place of rest.
Ask him to refresh and renew
your heart there.*

Psalm 148:1 MGE

'Praise Him from the mountain tops!'

Find a place to call your mountain.
Go there just to praise God!
Praise him for those times
when you have felt as if you were
on the top of the world!

Acts 16:25

'About midnight Paul and Silas were praying and singing hymns to God, and the other prisoners were listening to them.'

Praise God
for the times in your life when he has brought you through impossible situations. Ask God to work mighty miracles in any current crisis that chains you in.

Psalm 147:4 MGE

'He counts the stars
and assigns each a name.'

Praise God
*that because he cares enough to name a
star, you can be sure that he cares enough
to bring light into your times of darkness.*

Psalm 147:3 MGE

'He heals the broken-hearted
and bandages their wounds.'

Praise God
*that whenever you feel your heart is broken,
he is there with healing and hope.
Invite him to cradle you in his arms of love.*

Psalm 146:10 MGE

'God's in charge – always.
Zion's God is God for good. Hallelujah!'

Praise God
*when things do not work out the way
in which you would like them to,
because God is still in control!*

Psalm 147:1

'Praise the Lord. How good it is to sing praises to our God, how pleasant and fitting to praise him!'

Begin your day with beauty.
Praise God for all that he means to you!

Psalm 147:5 MGE

'Our Lord is great with limitless strength.
We'll never comprehend what
he knows and does.'

Praise God
*that we can live with his
stupendous strength in our lives,
when we sincerely surrender
our strength to him.*

Romans 8:28

'And we know that in all things God works for the good of those who love him, who have been called according to his purpose.'

Praise God
*that he is committed to taking
your disappointments
and to turning them into
something good for you!*

Psalm 149:1 GNB

'Praise the Lord! Sing a new song to the Lord; praise him in the assembly of his faithful people!'

Praise God
that he is worth talking about!
Share your delight in God with others
who care about him too.

Psalm 123:1 MGE

'I look to you, heaven-dwelling God,
look up to you for help.'

Praise God
*that when you need help,
you only need to raise your
head and heart heavenwards.*

Psalm 116:5 MGE

'God is gracious – it is he who makes things right, our most compassionate God.'

Praise God
*that even though we mess up at times,
he is able to make things right.*

Psalm 47:1 NLT

'Come, everyone, and clap your hands for joy! Shout to God with joyful praise!'

*Get on your feet and give God
a round of applause!
Praise him for those who bring joy and
laughter into your life.*

Psalm 32:11

'Rejoice in the Lord and be glad, you righteous; sing, all you who are upright in heart!'

When we are at one with God, our hearts can truly appreciate his goodness. Hand your heart over to God and then praise him!

1 Thessalonians 5:16-18

'Be joyful always; pray continually;
give thanks in all circumstances, for this is
God's will for you in Christ Jesus.'

Praise God
that when we thank him,
we can know that we are
completely connected to his heart.

Psalm 68:19

'Praise be to the Lord, to God our Saviour, who daily bears our burdens.'

Praise God
that there is no heartache you will have to deal with on your own. Each day he comes and invites you to surrender your struggles to him.

Psalm 16:7

'I will praise the Lord, who counsels me,
even at night my heart instructs me.'

Praise God
*that when you are asleep,
he is awake,
speaking to your heart.
Ask God to help you to listen for his voice.*

Revelation 4:8

' "Holy, holy, holy is the Lord God Almighty,
who was, and is, and is to come!" '

Praise God
*for being in your past, your present
and your future.
Ask him to enable you to live
your life humbled by his holiness.*

Revelation 5:12

' "Worthy is the Lamb, who was slain, to receive power and wealth and wisdom and strength and honour and glory and praise!" '

*If you don't know what to praise God for – remember there is always Calvary!
As you think of Jesus' broken body on the cross, ask God to heal your broken heart from sin.*

Luke 8:24

'He got up and rebuked the wind and the raging waters; the storm subsided, and all was calm.'

Praise God
*that no storm is stronger than his power to create calm out of chaos.
Beckon God to take control of any storm that you are wrestling with right now.*

Isaiah 43:19

' "See I am doing a new thing!
Now it springs up; do you not perceive it?
I am making a way in the desert
and streams in the wasteland." '

Praise God
*that he is able to make a way
when all seems dead and lifeless.
Pray for those you know who are going
through dry, depressing times, that they
will see swirling streams of hope
in their struggles.*

2 Timothy 1:7

'For God did not give us a spirit of timidity,
but a spirit of power, of love
and of self-discipline.'

Praise God
*that when we are in situations
that cause us to want to hide,
he enables us to meet them with
his confidence, his loving actions
and his self-control.*

Philippians 4:13

'I can do everything through him who gives me strength.'

Praise God
*that his strength is ours –
if we ask him for it!*

Psalm 55:22

'Cast your cares on the Lord and he will sustain you; he will never let the righteous fall.'

Praise God
*that he is able to hold us up
when we feel like falling down.
Ask God to present you with his peace
as you place your problems
in the palms of his hands.*

Isaiah 40:29-31

'He gives strength to the weary
and increases the power of the weak.
Even youths grow tired and weary, and
young men stumble and fall; but those who
hope in the Lord will renew their strength.
They will soar on wings like eagles;
they will run and not grow weary,
they will walk and not be faint.'

Praise God
that even though we get weary, he never will.
Sit still.
*Ask God to pour his hope into you so that in
your heart you may fly like an eagle!*

Nehemiah 8:10

' "The joy of the Lord is your strength." '

Praise God
*that his joy can be your motivation
when your life has no laughter.
Invite God to deposit his joy in your heart.*

Philippians 4:19

'And my God will meet all your needs according to his glorious riches in Christ Jesus.'

Praise God
that he is richly resourceful in taking care of our needs.
Ask him to supply you with a heart's supply of contentment while you wait for your needs to be met in the very best way.

Jeremiah 31:3

'The Lord appeared to us in the past, saying:
"I have loved you with an everlasting love;
I have drawn you with loving-kindness." '

Praise God
*that he has always been there for you
and that he always will be.
Ask him to help you experience
his love in your heart.*

Deuteronomy 31:8

' "The Lord himself goes before you and will
be with you; he will never leave you
nor forsake you. Do not be afraid;
do not be discouraged." '

Praise God
*that loneliness need not absorb your heart
– for God himself has chosen to be your
constant companion.*

2 Corinthians 12:9

' "My grace is sufficient for you, for my power is made perfect in weakness." '

Praise God
that your weakness is God's opportunity to show what his power can do for you. Tell God that you want to make room for his power in your life.

Isaiah 43:25

' "I, even I, am he who blots out your transgressions, for my own sake, and remembers your sins no more." '

Praise God
that when it comes to our sins, he chooses to treat us as if we have done no wrong.
Be free today,
knowing that your mistakes of yesterday,
do not have to be your 'baggage' of today.

1 Corinthians 10:13

'And God is faithful; he will not let you be tempted beyond what you can bear. But when you are tempted, he will also provide a way out, so that you can stand up under it.'

Praise God
*that every tough situation we go through leads to a 'way out' sign.
Ask God to help you to be patient until you get there.*

Matthew 11:28-30

' "Come to me, all you who are weary and
burdened, and I will give you rest.
Take my yoke upon you and learn from me,
for I am gentle and humble in heart,
and you will find rest for your souls.
For my yoke is easy and my burden is light." '

Praise God
*that he understands the pressures and
problems that plague us.
Praise God
that he presents us with the perfect solution –
his ability to shoulder our strongest struggles.
Give him permission to do just that!*

Psalm 18:39

'You armed me with strength for battle.'

Praise God
*that we are not left defenceless
against the enemy.
Stand still so that God can place his
armour upon you.*

Psalm 90:14

'Satisfy us in the morning with your unfailing love, that we may sing for joy and be glad all our days.'

Praise God
*that he wakes us each morning with
a hug heavy with love.
Ask God to let his love cause you to live
with joy in your heart
and a smile on your face.*

1 John 3:1

'How great is the love the Father has lavished on us, that we should be called children of God! And that is what we are!'

Praise God
*that he invites us to call him Father
and that he calls us his children.
Ask God to help you to feel 'rich' today,
simply because you are his daughter.*

Jeremiah 33:3

' "Call to me and I will answer you and tell you great and unsearchable things you do not know." '

Praise God
*that he not only invites us to talk with him,
but he promises to listen and answer.
Pray that as you talk with God
your understanding, respect and
passion for him will grow.*

Jeremiah 32:27

*' "I am the Lord, the God of all mankind.
Is anything too hard for me?" '*

Praise God
*that no situation, no problem, no anxiety,
no dilemma is too hard for him.
Be confident that as you talk with God
this morning, he is able to
deal with your concerns.*

2 Samuel 22:29

' "You are my lamp, O Lord; the Lord turns my darkness into light." '

Praise God
*that he is our personal flashlight
when our world turns dark.
Ask him to turn on the light
so that you can see clearly
which way to go.*

Ecclesiastes 3:11

'He has also set eternity in the
hearts of men.'

Praise God
*that we will all be lonely for God
until we invite him to take his
place in our hearts.
Spend time urging God to speak to those
you know who have a God-shaped
hole in their hearts.*

Isaiah 30:18

'Yet the Lord longs to be gracious to you;
he rises to show you compassion.'

Praise God
*that he has loving thoughts towards you.
With gratitude ask God to minister to you
in gentle and generous ways.*

Isaiah 30:19

'How gracious he will be when you cry
for help! As soon as he hears,
he will answer you.'

Praise God
*that the moment you cry out to him,
he has provided an answer.
Remind God to keep you aware of that as
you wait to see the answer for yourself.*

Psalm 94:18, 19

'When I said "My foot is slipping," your love,
O Lord, supported me. When anxiety was
great within me, your consolation
brought joy to my soul.'

Praise God
*that his love is strong enough to hold us,
when we feel we are weak.
Ask God to take the anxiety that
somersaults inside of you
and to be your comforter.*

2 Chronicles 20:15

' "Do not be afraid or discouraged because of this vast army. For this battle is not yours, but God's." '

Praise God
*that the main battle we have to fight is the one where we are challenged to trust him more than we trust ourselves.
Give God any other battles that are threatening to overwhelm you.*

Psalm 81:16

'With honey from the rock I would satisfy you.'

Praise God
*that he is able to provide sweetness
when we least expect it.
Open your heart to God and ask him
to satisfy you as he promises.*

Matthew 6:8

' "Your Father knows what you need before you ask him." '

Praise God
*that whatever your need,
big or small, trivial or important,
your Father in Heaven is aware of it
and he will do something about it!*

Psalm 119:164

'Seven times a day I praise you for your righteous laws.'

Like a challenge?
Praise God today seven times
and tomorrow too,
and who knows, you may want to do it
more and more and more. . . .

Psalm 135:3

'Praise the Lord, for the Lord is good;
sing praise to his name, for that is pleasant.'

*Want to start the day in the best possible way?
Then start praising God and you'll soon start
to feel good.*

Psalm 107:8

'Let them give thanks to the Lord for his unfailing love and his wonderful deeds for men.'

Don't know what to praise God for? Think about all the things that are right about him.

Joel 2:26

' "And you will praise the name
of the Lord your God,
who has worked wonders for you." '

Praise God
*that he is always at work on your behalf
– even when you are not aware of it.
Ask God to keep your eyes open to see the
exciting things he is doing for you.*

Psalm 68:19 *KJV*

'Blessed be the Lord, who daily loadeth us with benefits.'

Praise God
that every day he meets us with an armful of blessings!
Greet him with open arms to receive them!

2 Corinthians 2:14 KJV

'Now thanks be unto God, which always causeth us to triumph in Christ.'

Praise God
that the words 'failure' or 'defeat' do not have a place in your relationship with him. Ask God to help you to stand tall, confident that you are a winner because of Jesus Christ!

Luke 1:37

' "Nothing is impossible with God." '

Praise God
*that with him the impossible
is always possible.
Challenge God to do the amazing for you!*

2 Corinthians 1:3, 4

'Praise be to the God and Father of our Lord Jesus Christ, the Father of compassion and the God of all comfort, who comforts us in all our troubles, so that we can comfort those in any trouble with the comfort we ourselves have received from God.'

Praise God
*that we face no sorrow without God's arms warmly wrapped around us.
Spend time asking God to comfort those whom you know are sad.*

Psalm 23:1

'The Lord is my shepherd,
I shall not be in want.'

Praise God
*that he will take care of your every need
as diligently as a shepherd
takes care of his sheep.
Share with the Good Shepherd your wants
and the wants of your fellow sheep.*

1 Corinthians 2:9

' "No eye has seen, no ear has heard, no mind has conceived what God has prepared for those who love him." '

Praise God
that your imagination is no match for his reality to come.

Psalm 28:6

'Praise be to the Lord, for he has heard my cry for mercy.'

Praise God
that he is always listening out for your voice just as a mother listens for the cry of her newborn baby.
Ask God to touch you with his kindness and compassion.

John 8:4, 5

They 'said to Jesus, "Teacher, this woman was caught in the act of adultery. In the Law Moses commanded us to stone such women. Now what do you say?" '

Remember that even though some may have a hard time forgiving you when you have done wrong – God never does!
Praise him for that!

Exodus 15:2

' "The Lord is my strength and my song;
he has become my salvation. He is my God,
and I will praise him, my father's God, and
I will exalt him." '

Praise God
*that in him you have everything you need –
strength when you are weak
a song when you are sad
salvation when you sin
a God when you are without hope
a Father when you are lonely.*

Isaiah 25:1

'O Lord, you are my God; I will exalt you and praise your name, for in perfect faithfulness you have done marvellous things, things planned long ago.'

Praise God
*that he is always committed to
doing what he says
and that what he does is always astounding!*

Psalm 71:14

'But as for me, I shall always have hope;
I will praise you more and more.'

Praise God
that as he keeps on giving us hope and we keep on receiving it – we will regularly have something to praise him for!

1 Chronicles 16:25

'For great is the Lord and most worthy of praise; he is to be feared above all gods.'

Praise God
for all the worthwhile things he has done for you.

Revelation 21:3

'And I heard a loud voice from the throne saying, "Now the dwelling of God is with men, and he will live with them. They will be his people, and God himself will be with them and be their God."'

Praise God
that his dream is to spend eternity with you!

2 Chronicles 20:21

'Jehoshaphat appointed men to sing to the Lord and to praise him for the splendour of his holiness as they went out at the head of the army saying, "Give thanks . . .".'

Praise God
that he is different from us because he is holy. Ask God to help you to appreciate his holiness.

Daniel 2:20

' "Praise be to the name of God for ever and ever; wisdom and power are his." '

Praise God
that two of the things we seek in life –
power to achieve what is important
and wisdom to know what is valuable –
can be found in him.
Be at peace knowing that his power and his
wisdom are available to you.

Jeremiah 29:11

' "For I know the plans I have for you," declares the Lord, "plans to prosper you and not to harm you, plans to give you hope and a future." '

Praise God
*that his plans for your life will always be more satisfying than your own.
Ask God to reach out to the hearts of those who live with hopelessness.*

1 John 4:4

'The one who is in you is greater than the one who is in the world.'

Praise God
*that he, and all he represents,
is more important
than what is seen as valuable
in this world.*

Psalm 62:1

'My soul finds rest in God alone.'

Praise God
that he is our ultimate soul mate.

Luke 12:7

' "Indeed, the very hairs of your head are all numbered. Don't be afraid; you are worth more than many sparrows." '

Praise God
*that focusing on his love
will help take your eyes off
those things that you are afraid of.*

Isaiah 49:1

'Before I was born the Lord called me;
from my birth he has made mention
of my name.'

Praise God
*that he has a special place for you
– and that is in his heart!*

2 Corinthians 6:18

' "I will be a Father to you, and you shall be my sons and daughters, says the Lord Almighty." '

Praise God
that his greatest joy is to be your Father.
Make it your greatest joy to be
his daughter.

Isaiah 63:16

'You, O Lord, are our Father,
our Redeemer from of old is your name.'

Praise God
*that he is a Father
who never fails
and a Redeemer
who never ceases to forgive.*

Proverbs 3:6

'In all your ways acknowledge him, and he will make your paths straight.'

Praise God
*that when we recognise him as an
expert planner in our lives,
we will never have to
live with the confusion
of not knowing where we are headed.*

Jeremiah 30:17

' "But I will restore you to health and heal your wounds," declares the Lord.'

Praise God
*that he is able to do what you can never do:
give complete healing to every part of your life.*

Psalm 70:5

'You are my help and my deliverer.'

Praise God
that there is no situation that is beyond his assistance and rescue.

Psalm 118:5

'In my anguish I cried to the Lord, and he answered by setting me free.'

Praise God
*that our worries need not bind us,
if we share them with him.*

Romans 10:13

' "Everyone who calls on the name of the Lord will be saved." '

Praise God
*that eternity with him is possible
the moment we call out to him.*

Psalm 27:10

'Though my father and mother forsake me,
the Lord will receive me.'

Praise God
*that even though others may reject us,
he always accepts us.*

Psalm 30:5

'Weeping may remain for a night,
but rejoicing comes in the morning.'

Praise God
*that he has put a time limit on our crying.
Let's ask him for the dawn's light to come
into our sorrows.*

Isaiah 43:2

'When you pass through the waters,
I will be with you;
and when you pass through the rivers,
they will not sweep over you.
When you walk through the fire,
you shall not be burned;
the flames will not set you ablaze.'

Praise God
*that with him by your side,
no situation need suffocate your spirit.
Ask God to help you to be
aware of his hand in yours.*

Psalm 18:6

'In my distress I called to the Lord;
I cried to my God for help.
From his temple he heard my voice.'

Praise God
*that in the very heart of heaven he sits,
listening for your voice.
Cry out to him
from the very depths of your heart.*

Psalm 118:6

'The Lord is with me;
I will not be afraid.
What can man do to me?'

Praise God
that when he walks beside us
there is no room for fear as well.
We can be confident that he is capable
of conquering our concerns.

Psalm 34:4

'I sought the Lord, and he answered me;
he delivered me from all my fears.'

Praise God
*that every fear that is prominent
in our lives takes a back seat
when we cry out to him.*

Isaiah 41:9

' "I have chosen you and have not rejected you." '

Praise God
that we can always know that we have a place in his heart and in his dreams.

Psalm 34:19

'A righteous man may have many troubles,
but the Lord delivers him from them all.'

Praise God
*that even though life is full of frustrations,
God is full of fresh ideas to deal with them!*

Psalm 25:8

'Good and upright is the Lord.'

Praise God
*that everything that is precious, positive
and promising is part of him.*

Psalm 118:8

'Take refuge in the Lord.'

Praise God
that he is always one step ahead of us,
one step to the side of us
and one step behind us
– for now and for eternity.

1 Corinthians 15:58

'Stand firm. Let nothing move you. Always give yourselves fully to the work of the Lord, because you know that your labour in the Lord is not in vain.'

Praise God
that whatever we do for God
will always be successful
– even when we think we have failed!

Micah 4:2

' "Come, let us go up to the mountain of the Lord, to the house of the God of Jacob. He will teach us his ways, so that we may walk in his paths." '

Praise God
that time spent with him will cause us to value his ways and to live them in our lives.

Psalm 139:2, 3

'You know when I sit and when I rise;
you perceive my thoughts from afar.
You discern my going out and my lying
down; you are familiar with all my ways.'

Praise God
*that he knows us inside out –
and he still loves us!*

Psalm 138:3

'When I called, you answered me;
you made me bold and stout-hearted.'

Praise God
that he is able to make you strong enough
on the inside so that you and he can tackle
your problems on the outside.

Exodus 33:14

' "My Presence will go with you, and I will give you rest." '

Praise God
that his personal pledge to you
is that his presence will provide you
with his peace.

Lamentations 3:25

'The Lord is good to those whose hope is in him, to the one who seeks him.'

Praise God
*that patience in him
will always be rewarded with
great things from him.*

Psalm 27:14

'Wait for the Lord; be strong and take heart and wait for the Lord.'

Praise God
*that when we are still before him
he is able to fill our minds with courage
and our hearts with strength.*

Romans 5:5

'And hope does not disappoint us, because God has poured out his love into our hearts by the Holy Spirit, whom he has given us.'

Praise God
*that
his love in our hearts,
gives us
his hope in our lives.*

Psalm 22:5

'They cried to you and were saved; in you they trusted and were not disappointed.'

Praise God
*that when we completely put our confidence in him,
we will no longer be destroyed by disappointments.*

Psalm 138:8

'The Lord will fulfil his purpose for me.'

Praise God
*that everything that concerns you,
concerns him.
Ask him to fulfil his purpose
in those areas in your life
that cause you pain.*

Ephesians 4:32

'Be kind and compassionate to one another, forgiving each other, just as in Christ God forgave you.'

Praise God
*that forgiveness from God to us
means that there can be
forgiveness from us to others.*

***Isaiah 53**:4 KJV*

'Surely he has borne our griefs,
and carried our sorrows.'

Praise God
*that he seeks to take our sadness,
sorrows and struggles
and carry them away.*

Isaiah 60:19, 20

'For the Lord will be your everlasting light,
and your God will be your glory. . . .
and your days of sorrow will end.'

Praise God
*that the blazing brightness
he brings into our lives
will never be extinguished.*

Psalm 119:50

'My comfort in my sufferings is this:
Your promise preserves my life.'

Praise God
*that his written word can speak to us
as nothing else can.
Ask God to cause you to hunger
to read his Bible.*

2 Timothy 4:18

'The Lord will rescue me from every evil attack and will bring me safely to his heavenly kingdom. To him be glory for ever and ever.'

Praise God
that he rescues us from the ravages of evil and prepares us to live with him in heaven.

2 Corinthians 5:17

'If anyone is in Christ, he is a new creation; the old has gone, the new has come!'

Praise God
*that with him our past is truly forgiven
and our future is truly fantastic!*

Psalm 84:11

'The Lord God is a sun and shield;
the Lord bestows favour and honour;
no good thing does he withhold
from those whose walk is blameless.'

Praise God
*that he is as warm and welcoming
as the sun's rays and
as strong and secure as a shield.
Ask God to help you walk with him.*

Psalm 118:24

'This is the day the Lord has made;
let us rejoice and be glad in it.'

Praise God
*that each day declares
the creative power of God.
Pray that you will be able to rejoice
in the gift of each new day.*

Romans 8:38, 39

'For I am convinced that neither death nor life, neither angels nor demons, neither the present nor the future, nor any powers, neither height nor depth, nor anything else in all creation, will be able to separate us from the love of God that is in Christ Jesus our Lord.'

Praise God
that his love for us cannot be quenched by anything.

Isaiah 60:2

' "The Lord rises upon you
and his glory appears over you." '

Praise God
*that his friendship with you
can be seen by others.*

Micah 7:8
'Though I have fallen I will rise.
Though I sit in darkness,
the Lord will be my light.'

Praise God
that no matter how 'sunless' our situation,
he will always be our source of 'sunshine'.

John 14:27

' "Peace I leave with you; my peace I give you. I do not give to you as the world gives. Do not let your hearts be troubled and do not be afraid." '

Praise God
that his peace is unique.
Ask him to give you a smidgeon of that today.

2 Timothy 2:13

'If we are faithless, he will remain faithful,
for he cannot disown himself.'

Praise God
*that even though we are not consistent
in our response to him,
he is always constant
in the way he deals with us.*

Psalm 25:14

'The Lord confides in those who fear him;
he makes his covenant known to them.'

Praise God
*that he wants such an intimate
relationship with us
that he shares his confidences with us.*

2 Corinthians 1:9

'But this happened that we might not rely on ourselves but on God.'

Praise God
for any situation that causes us to depend upon him more than ourselves. Ask God to help you experience the satisfaction of depending upon him.

2 Peter 1:3

'His divine power has given us everything
we need for life and godliness.'

Praise God
*that to approach life
with a godly attitude we just need
to ask for his power.*

Luke 15:20

' "But while he was still a long way off,
his father saw him and was filled with
compassion for him; he ran to his son,
threw his arms around him
and kissed him." '

__Praise God__
*that he yearns for the moment when he can
wrap his arms about us and
welcome us home.
What delightful love!*

James 5:11

'You have heard of Job's perseverance and have seen what the Lord finally brought about. The Lord is full of compassion and mercy.'

Praise God
that the hard times in our lives will always be followed by times of unimaginable blessing!

James 1:5

'If any of you lacks wisdom, he should ask God, who gives generously to all without finding fault, and it will be given to him.'

Praise God
*that we have a guaranteed source
of wisdom in him.
Seek God's wisdom right now.*

Philippians 4:6 MGE

'Don't fret or worry. Instead of worrying, pray. Let petitions and praises shape your worries into prayers, letting God know your concerns.'

Praise God
that when we praise him we can be sure that he can find solutions to our problems. Do just as God says and pray your worries away!

Philippians 3:8

'What is more, I consider everything a loss compared to the surpassing greatness of knowing Christ Jesus my Lord, for whose sake I have lost all things.'

Praise God
that knowing him is our greatest delight in life.

Matthew 7:11

' "If you, then, though you are evil,
know how to give good gifts to your children,
how much more will your Father in heaven
give good gifts to those who ask him!" '

Praise God
*that, as our Father, he will always
give us the best!*

John 6:35

' "I am the bread of life. He who comes to me will never go hungry, and he who believes in me will never be thirsty."'

Praise God
that our longing of him in our hearts will always be met.

Job 36:24, 25, CIV

'Remember to praise his [God's] work . . . .
Everybody has seen it.'

Praise God
*that his great works can be seen
by everyone who looks –
especially with the heart.*

Ruth 2:20, CIV

'The Lord still continues to be kind
to all people!'

Praise God
*for his wonderful kindness to the children
of men and women;
it will bless us for ever and ever.*

Job 36:26, CIV

'God is so great! He is greater than we can understand!'

Praise God
*that though he is greater than
we can ever understand,
he sent Jesus to help us see
just how great he is!*

***Job 19:25,* NKJV**

'I know that my Redeemer lives,
and he shall stand at last on the earth.'

Praise God
*that our Redeemer lives
and has promised to come again
for those who love him.
How we long to see him!*